FAITH

and

Modernity

Dr. Mario Joseph

ISBN 979-8-89243-627-4 (paperback)
ISBN 979-8-89243-628-1 (digital)

Christian Faith Publishing
832 Park Avenue
Meadville, PA 16335
www.christianfaithpublishing.com

Printed in the United States of America

In this journey called life, I stand on the shoulders of giants, surrounded by a constellation of love, guidance, and support. With deep gratitude, I extend my heartfelt acknowledgment to those who have been instrumental in shaping my path and enriching my existence.

Idovia Jean Pierre, you are more than a mentor. You are a beacon of wisdom and inspiration, illuminating my way with your guidance and encouragement.

Suzanne Jean Pierre, my cherished adopted mother and guardian angel, your unconditional love has been my sanctuary, nurturing my soul and uplifting my spirit through every trial and triumph.

Nelly Theodat, my dearest friend and beloved mom, your unwavering friendship and maternal affection have been a source of strength and joy, grounding me in love and laughter.

Yvanne Bros, Bertha Appolon, and Alphone Altidor, you are my real-life mentors. Your wisdom and guidance have sculpted my character and fueled my aspirations.

Jean Patrick and Carole Revolus, instruments of divine intervention, your presence has transformed the seasons of my life, leading me toward growth, purpose, and fulfillment.

To my parents, Lamercie Bouquets and Joseph Pauleus Joseph, your boundless love and sacrifices have laid the foundation of my existence, instilling in me the values of resilience, integrity, and compassion.

To my perfect and beautiful wife, Rolaine, and our children, Romario, Darnell, Rollinsky, Andrew, and Matthew Joseph, you embody love's purest essence, filling my days with immeasurable joy and purpose.

To my beloved brothers, sisters, and the congregation of Bethel, your unwavering support and fellowship have enriched my journey, infusing it with warmth, camaraderie, and spiritual nourishment.

To the esteemed leaders and congregation of Bethel, Rev. Dr. Older Azard, Rev. Dr. Fenell Gratia, and Bishop Englade Destra, your guidance and spiritual stewardship have been a guiding light, illuminating my path with faith, hope, and divine wisdom.

And to all our cherished friends, near and far, your presence has been a constant source of laughter, companionship, and shared memories, enriching the tapestry of my life in countless ways.

Each of you holds a precious place in the mosaic of my existence, and I am eternally grateful for that.

My journey in faith has been marked by various roles, from serving as the president of the board of trustees and administration at Bethel Haitian Baptist Church to founding and coordinating the Epic Youth Nations. My academic pursuits, spanning from Biblical Study to Business and technology, have always been guided by one purpose: to bridge the gap between faith and modernity.

In today's rapidly evolving world, the challenge of reconciling traditional Christian beliefs with modern societal values and technological advancements is one that many believers grapple with. How do we, as followers of Christ, navigate the complexities of a digital age and stay true to the timeless teachings of the Bible? How do we engage with modern society without compromising our core beliefs?

Faith and Modernity is an exploration of these questions and more. This book is not just a theoretical discourse but a practical guide, drawing from the rich tapestry of Christian teachings and the realities of the twenty-first century. It reflects my journey, struggles, and revelations as I sought to understand God's purpose in a world dominated by technology and changing societal norms.

As you explore these pages, I pray that you find clarity, inspiration, and a renewed sense of purpose. May this book serve as an inspiration, guiding you through the challenges and opportunities that come with living a life of faith in a modern world.

CONTENTS

CHAPTER 1

Setting the Stage

In the vast tapestry of human history, faith has been a guiding light for countless souls seeking purpose, comfort, and understanding. The Bible, a cornerstone of Christian belief, has been a source of wisdom and guidance for millennia. As we stand at the crossroads of faith and modernity, it's essential to understand the historical context of this relationship and how the teachings of the Bible remain relevant in our rapidly changing world. "Jesus Christ is the same yesterday and today and or ever" (Hebrews 13:8). This verse reminds us of the unchanging nature of Christ and His teachings.

While societies evolve and technologies advance, the core tenets of Christianity remain steadfast. This constancy offers solace to believers in a world that often feels transient and fleeting. The relationship between faith and societal progress is intricate. Historically, Christianity has been both a catalyst for change and a bastion of tradition. The early Christian church, for instance, was revolutionary in its teachings of love, equality, and forgiveness. These teachings challenged the societal norms of the time and laid the groundwork for many modern values. "There is neither Jew nor Gentile, neither slave nor free, nor is there male and female, for you are all one in Christ Jesus" (Galatians 3:28).

This latter verse underscores the revolutionary idea of equality in the eyes of God, a concept that was radical during Apostle Paul's time and remains a guiding principle in modern discussions about equality and human rights. However, as societies progressed, there were times when the church resisted certain aspects of modernity, often out of a desire to preserve religious traditions. The tension between faith and progress is not new; it has been a recurring theme throughout history.

The Renaissance, the Enlightenment, and the Industrial Revolution posed challenges and opportunities for the Christian faith. "Do not conform to the pattern of this world but be transformed by the renewing of your mind. Then you will be able to test and approve what God's will is—his good, pleasing and perfect will" (Romans 12:2). This verse from Romans advises believers to remain steadfast in their faith and not be swayed by societal pressures. It encourages introspection and a deep understanding of God's will, even in the face of modern challenges.

The pace of change is unprecedented in the twenty-first century. We live in a world of instant communication, artificial intelligence, and space exploration. Yet the Bible continues to be a source of guidance, its verses offering insights that are surprisingly relevant to contemporary dilemmas. "It is the glory of God to conceal a matter; to search out a matter is the glory of kings" (Proverbs 25:2). This Proverb celebrates the pursuit of knowledge, suggesting that humans are encouraged to seek understanding while God knows all. It's a reminder that faith and curiosity can coexist and that modernity's quest for knowledge is, in many ways, a reflection of God's design.

As we navigate the complexities of faith in a modern world, the Bible serves as a compass, its verses lighting the path. The historical relationship between religion and societal progress is a testament to Christianity's adaptability and enduring relevance.

CHAPTER 2

The Evolution of Faith in a Modern World

The journey of faith is as old as humanity itself. From the earliest days of creation to the bustling modern age, faith has been an inspiration, guiding individuals and communities through the challenges and triumphs of existence. With its rich tapestry of stories, teachings, and prophecies, the Bible has been a foundational guide for Christians. A look at the evolution of faith in our contemporary era is essential to reflect on how biblical teachings have informed and shaped this journey. "In the beginning was the Word, and the Word was with God, and the Word was God" (John 1:1). This profound verse from the Gospel of John emphasizes the eternal nature of God's Word. While the world changes, the Word remains a constant, unchanging force. This continuity provides a foundation for faith to evolve without losing its essence.

Throughout history, significant events have challenged and reshaped religious beliefs. The Renaissance, with its emphasis on humanism, the Scientific Revolution, which brought forth a new understanding of the universe, and the social and political upheavals of the twentieth century, all posed questions about the nature of faith and its place in a changing world. "For now we see only a reflection as in a mirror; then we shall see face to face. Now I know in part; then I shall know fully, even as I am fully known" (1 Corinthians 13:12). The apostle Paul acknowledges in his letter to the Corinthians, the limitations of human understanding. As we gain knowledge and experience societal shifts, our understanding of faith also evolves.

Yet the promise remains that one day, all will be revealed in its entirety. The impact of scientific discoveries on faith has been particularly significant. The heliocentric model, the theory of evolution, and advances in medical science have all prompted deep theological reflections and sometimes tensions. Yet the Bible offers wisdom that can bridge the perceived gap between faith and science. "The heavens declare the glory of God; the skies proclaim the work of his hands" (Psalm 19:1). This Psalm celebrates the wonders of creation, suggesting that nature is a testament to God's majesty. Rather than diminishing faith, scientific discoveries can deepen our awe and appreciation of the Creator.

In the modern age, globalization and technological advancements have brought diverse cultures and beliefs closer than ever before. This interconnectedness offers both challenges and opportunities for the evolution of faith. How does one remain faithful to Christian teachings while respecting and understanding diverse perspectives? "I have become all things to all people so that by all possible means I might save some" (1 Corinthians 9:22). Paul's approach to evangelism was one of adaptability and understanding. In a globalized world, this verse serves as a reminder of the importance of empathy and open-mindedness in sharing the Christian message.

The evolution of faith in the modern world is a journey of reflection, adaptation, and growth. While the challenges of modernity are accurate, the Bible offers timeless wisdom and guidance. By grounding ourselves in scripture and approaching the world with an open heart, we can navigate the complexities of our age with grace and conviction.

CHAPTER 3

Technology and Faith

In the annals of human history, few things have transformed society as profoundly as technology. From the invention of the wheel to the digital revolution, technological advancements have reshaped how we live, work, and connect. As Christians, the intersection of faith and technology prompts reflection on how we can integrate these tools into our spiritual journey while staying faithful to biblical teachings.

> Every good and perfect gift is from above, coming down from the Father of the heavenly lights, who does not change like shifting shadows. (James 1:17)

This verse from James reminds us that all advancements, including technology, are gifts from God. They are tools to be used for humanity's betterment and glorify God's name. The digital age has brought with it a plethora of opportunities for believers. Online platforms have enabled the gospel to reach corners of the world previously inaccessible. Virtual churches, Bible study apps, and Christian podcasts have made spiritual resources available at the touch of a button. "Go into all the world and preach the gospel to all creation" (Mark 16:15). Jesus's Great Commission to his disciples resonates with renewed vigor in the internet age.

Technology has amplified the reach of evangelism, allowing Christians to fulfill this mandate innovatively. However, with these opportunities come challenges. The virtual world's endless information and distractions can sometimes lead to spiritual detachment. The essence of community, so central to Christian fellowship can feel diluted in online spaces. "Let us not give up meeting together, as some are in the habit of doing, but encouraging one another— and all the more as you see the Day approaching" (Hebrews 10:25). While virtual worship has its place, this verse from Hebrews underscores the importance of physical fellowship. It's a reminder to strike a balance, using technology to complement, not replace, traditional forms of worship and community.

Another challenge posed by technology is the ethical dilemmas it presents. Artificial intelligence, bioengineering, and data privacy are areas where Christians must grapple with moral questions. "Behold, I send you out as sheep amid wolves. Therefore, be wise as serpents and harmless as doves" (Matthew 10:16). In navigating the complexities of the modern tech landscape, Jesus's advice to his disciples offers guidance.

Christians are called to approach technology with discernment, ensuring their actions align with biblical principles. Furthermore, the digital age, with its emphasis on instant gratification can sometimes lead to a diminished capacity for patience and reflection, virtues extolled in the Bible. "But those who wait on the Lord Shall renew their strength; They shall mount up with wings like eagles, they shall run and not be weary, They shall walk and not faint" (Isaiah 40:31). In a world of constant notifications and updates, this verse from Isaiah is a poignant reminder of the strength and renewal that comes from pausing, reflecting, and waiting on the Lord.

In all its marvel and complexity, technology offers Christians both challenges and opportunities. By grounding ourselves in Scripture and approaching technological advancements with discernment and wisdom, we can harness these tools for God's glory. The fusion of faith and technology is not a divergence but a testament to the adaptability and resilience of the Christian journey in the modern age.

CHAPTER 4

Modern Ethics and Morality

The ever-evolving landscape of modern society continually presents new ethical and moral dilemmas. From bioethical concerns surrounding genetic engineering to debates on social justice, the questions of right and wrong have never been more complex. As Christians, the Bible serves as our moral compass, guiding our decisions and actions in this intricate world.

> He has shown you, O mortal, what is good. And what does the Lord require of you? To act justly and to love mercy and to walk humbly with your God. (Micah 6:8)

This verse from Micah encapsulates the essence of Christian ethics: justice, mercy, and humility. These timeless principles provide a foundation for navigating modern moral challenges.

One of the most pressing ethical issues of our time is the advancement of medical science. Genetic editing, cloning, and assisted reproductive technologies raise profound questions about the sanctity of life and the limits of human intervention.

> For you created my inmost being; you knit me together in my mother's womb. I praise you because I am fearfully and wonderfully made; your works are wonderful; I know that full well. (Psalm 139:13–14)

This Psalm celebrates the divine craftsmanship inherent in every human being. It serves as a reminder of the sanctity of life and the care with which we must approach advancements that alter the very fabric of human existence.

Another significant area of ethical consideration is the environment. As stewards of God's creation, Christians are called to care for the earth and all its inhabitants. "The earth is the Lord's, and everything in it, the world, and all who live in it" (Psalm 24:1). This verse underscores the idea that the earth is a divine gift entrusted to humanity. Modern challenges like climate change, deforestation, and pollution require a faith-based response rooted in respect for God's creation.

Social justice issues, from racial inequality to economic disparities, also demand ethical reflection. The Bible, emphasizing justice, love, and compassion, guides how Christians can advocate for a fairer world. "Learn to do right; seek justice. Defend the oppressed. Take up the cause of the fatherless; plead the case of the widow" (Isaiah 1:17). Isaiah's call to action is as relevant today as it was in ancient times. It's a clarion call for believers to be at the forefront of social justice movements, championing the rights of the marginalized and oppressed.

The digital age, with its myriad opportunities and challenges, also presents ethical dilemmas. Privacy, data security, and digital ethics require Christians to be discerning and conscientious in their online interactions. "Therefore, whatever you want men to do to you, do also to them, for this is the Law and the Prophets" (Matthew 7:12). Often referred to as the "Golden Rule," this teaching of Jesus is a guiding principle in all interactions, including digital ones. It's a reminder to treat others with respect and integrity in the physical and virtual realms.

With their intricate challenges, modern ethics and morality require a deep-rooted faith and a thorough understanding of biblical teachings. With its timeless wisdom, the Bible serves as a beacon, illuminating the path for Christians in a complex world. We can navigate the modern age with moral clarity and conviction by grounding our decisions in scripture and approaching dilemmas with prayerful consideration.

CHAPTER 5

Faith in a Pluralistic Society

The tapestry of our global society is richly woven with diverse cultures, beliefs, and traditions. Christians face challenges and opportunities in this pluralistic world where myriad faiths and philosophies coexist. How does one remain steadfast in Christian beliefs while engaging respectfully with many perspectives? With its timeless teachings on love, understanding, and unity, the Bible provides invaluable guidance. "There is neither Jew nor Gentile, neither slave nor free, nor is there male and female, for you are all one in Christ Jesus" (Galatians 3:28). This verse from Galatians underscores the universality of the Christian message. In Christ, all distinctions, and barriers dissolve, emphasizing every individual's inherent worth and equality.

Interfaith dialogues have become increasingly crucial in our interconnected world. Such exchanges promote understanding, dispel misconceptions, and foster mutual respect. Engaging in these dialogues, Christians can find common ground while sharing the unique tenets of their faith. "Let your conversation be always full of grace, seasoned with salt, so that you may know how to answer everyone" (Colossians 4:6). Paul's advice to the Colossians is a reminder to approach interfaith dialogues with grace and wisdom. Conversations should be respectful, insightful, and reflective of Christ's love.

However, living in a pluralistic society also presents challenges. The secularization of many societies can sometimes marginalize religious beliefs. Christians may face dilemmas in upholding their values in environments that may only occasionally be supportive or understanding. "Blessed are those who are persecuted because of righteousness, for theirs is the kingdom of heaven" (Matthew 5:10). Jesus's words during the Sermon on the Mount provide comfort and encouragement. They remind believers that challenges to their faith are not new and that enduring them with grace and conviction brings spiritual rewards.

Another aspect of living in a diverse society is the exposure to various cultural practices and celebrations. Participating in these can enrich our understanding and appreciation of humanity's vast tapestry. However, Christians must approach such engagements with discernment, ensuring they do not compromise their beliefs. "Test everything; hold fast what is good" (1 Thessalonians 5:21). Paul's counsel to the Thessalonians is apt for Christians navigating diverse cultural landscapes. It encourages believers to be open-minded yet discerning, holding onto what aligns with Christian values.

In a pluralistic society, Christians also have the unique opportunity to demonstrate Christ's love in action. By serving their communities, advocating for justice, and showing kindness to all, regardless of their beliefs, Christians can be living testimonies of their faith. "By this everyone will know that you are my disciples, if you love one another" (John 13:35). Jesus's words emphasize that love is the most potent testimony of faith. In a diverse world, actions often speak louder than words, and acts of love and service can bridge divides, fostering unity and understanding.

A pluralistic society, with its mosaic of beliefs and traditions, offers Christians a unique landscape to live out their faith. While challenges are inevitable, the Bible provides the wisdom and guidance to navigate them. By approaching the world with an open heart, grounded in Scripture, Christians can thrive in a diverse world, shining Christ's light for all to see.

CHAPTER 6

Secularism and Its Implications

In the modern age, the rise of secularism has profoundly impacted societies worldwide. Secularism, which emphasizes the separation of religion from civic affairs and public education, has challenged and reshaped faith's role in daily life. For Christians navigating this secular landscape, the Bible offers timeless insights and guidance on maintaining a vibrant confidence amidst shifting societal values. "But our citizenship is in heaven. And we eagerly await a Savior from there, the Lord Jesus Christ" (Philippians 3:20). Paul's words to the Philippians remind Christians that while they reside in this world, their ultimate allegiance is to a heavenly kingdom. This perspective helps believers maintain their faith in environments indifferent or hostile to religious beliefs.

The secularization of society has led to a more diverse range of opinions and values. While this diversity can enrich communities by promoting tolerance and understanding, it can also lead to a dilution of Christian principles in public discourse and policy. "Be on your guard; stand firm in the faith; be courageous; be strong" (1 Corinthians 16:13). Paul's exhortation to the Corinthians is a call to resilience. In the face of societal pressures to conform or dilute their beliefs, Christians are encouraged to stand firm, drawing strength from their faith.

One of the implications of secularism is the relegation of faith to the private sphere. Religion, once central to public life, is often viewed as a personal matter, separate from public discourse. This shift poses challenges for Christians seeking to integrate their faith

11

into every aspect of their lives. "In the same way, let your light shine before others, that they may see your good deeds and glorify your Father in heaven" (Matthew 5:16). Jesus's words during the Sermon on the Mount emphasize the importance of living out one's faith openly and authentically. Even in a secular society, believers are called to be a beacon of light, reflecting God's love through their actions and interactions.

Another implication of secularism is the questioning or rejecting of absolute moral truths. Morality can often be seen as relative in a secular worldview, leading to diverse interpretations of right and wrong. "Your word is a lamp for my feet, a light on my path" (Psalm 119:105). This Psalm highlights the Bible's role as a guiding force in the lives of believers. In a world of shifting morals, the Word of God provides a consistent and unchanging standard of truth. However, it's essential to recognize that secularism also offers opportunities for the Christian faith.

Faith becomes a personal choice in a society where religious beliefs are not imposed. This environment can lead to a more genuine and deeply-rooted faith, chosen out of personal conviction rather than societal obligation. "But in your hearts revere Christ as Lord. Always be prepared to give an answer to everyone who asks you to give the reason for the hope that you have. But do this with gentleness and respect" (1 Peter 3:15). Peter's advice underscores the importance of being ready to share one's faith, especially in a secular context. Engaging in respectful dialogue about beliefs can lead to deeper understanding and mutual respect.

While secularism presents challenges for Christians, it also offers opportunities for growth, reflection, and outreach. Grounded in the teachings of the Bible, believers can navigate the secular landscape with confidence, grace, and unwavering faith.

CHAPTER 7

Science, Medicine, and Religion

Science, medicine, and religion have often been perceived as distinct, sometimes conflicting. Yet, for many Christians, these fields harmoniously intertwine, each shedding light on the profound mysteries of existence. With its deep wisdom, the Bible offers insights that can help believers navigate the intricate dance between scientific discovery, medical advancement, and deep-rooted faith. "The heavens declare the glory of God; the skies proclaim the work of his hands." (Psalm 19:1) This Psalm beautifully encapsulates the idea that nature is a testament to God's grandeur. Every scientific discovery, from the vastness of the cosmos to the intricacies of DNA, can be seen as unveiling another facet of God's magnificent creation.

The realm of medicine, focusing on healing and alleviating suffering, resonates deeply with Christian teachings. Jesus, often called the "Great Physician," performed numerous healings, showcasing the divine value placed on health and well-being. "Heal the sick, raise the dead, cleanse those with leprosy, drive out demons. Freely you have received; freely give" (Matthew 10:8). Jesus's directive to His disciples underscores the importance of healing in His ministry. Modern medicine, with its myriad treatments and therapies, can be viewed as an extension of this divine mandate to heal and restore.

However, the rapid advancements in medical science, such as genetic engineering and bioethics, often present moral and ethical dilemmas. How do we balance the potential benefits of these technologies with the ethical concerns they raise? "I will instruct you and teach you in the way you should go; I will counsel you with my loving eye on you" (Psalm 32:8). In moments of uncertainty, this Psalm offers reassurance. God promises guidance and wisdom, helping believers navigate the complex decisions that medical advancements often entail.

The perceived dichotomy between science and religion has been debated for centuries. Some argue that science's empirical nature contrasts with religion's faith-based beliefs. However, many Christians view science as a tool to better understand the intricacies of God's creation. "For since the creation of the world, God's invisible qualities—his eternal power and divine nature—have been seen, being understood from what has been made, so that people are without excuse" (Romans 1:20). Paul's words to the Romans highlight that the natural world, which science seeks to understand, reflects God's character and attributes. Rather than detracting from faith, every scientific revelation can deepen our awe and wonder of the Creator.

Furthermore, the ethical principles that guide scientific and medical research resonate deeply with Christian values. The emphasis on preserving life, alleviating suffering, and seeking truth aligns with biblical teachings. "Do not be wise in your own eyes; fear the Lord and shun evil. This will bring health to your body and nourishment to your bones" (Proverbs 3:7–8). This Proverb emphasizes the importance of humility and reverence for God in all pursuits, including science and medicine. By approaching these fields with a heart attuned to God's wisdom, Christians can contribute positively, ensuring that advancements align with ethical and moral principles.

The intersections of science, medicine, and religion offer a rich tapestry of exploration, discovery, and faith. Grounded in the teachings of the Bible, Christians can engage in these fields with curiosity, ethics, and a deep sense of wonder, seeing in every discovery a reflection of the divine.

CHAPTER 8

The Role of Prayer in Modern Life

In the fast-paced rhythm of modern life, with its multitude of distractions and challenges, the ancient practice of prayer remains a beacon of solace and connection for many Christians. Prayer, a dialogue with the Divine offers believers a space of reflection, surrender, and communion. The Bible, with teachings and examples of worship, provides profound insights into its transformative power in contemporary contexts. "Do not be anxious about anything, but in every situation, by prayer and petition, with thanksgiving, present your requests to God" (Philippians 4:6). Paul's words to the Philippians are a timeless reminder of prayer's role as an antidote to anxiety. In an age of information overload and constant connectivity, prayer offers a sanctuary of peace, grounding believers in God's steadfast presence.

The modern world often emphasizes self-reliance and individualism. While these values have merits, they can sometimes lead to feelings of isolation and self-imposed pressure. Prayer, in contrast, is an act of humility and dependence on God. "Cast all your anxiety on him because he cares for you" (1 Peter 5:7). Peter's comforting words underscore the idea that God is not a distant entity but a loving Father eager to bear the burdens of His children. In moments of overwhelm, prayer becomes a conduit of surrender, a recognition of one's limitations, and a trust in divine providence.

The communal aspect of prayer, especially in group settings, fosters a sense of unity and shared purpose. Whether in church congregations, prayer groups, or family gatherings, collective prayer binds individuals in shared faith and intention. "For where two or three gather in my name, there am I with them" (Matthew 18:20). Jesus's affirmation of communal prayer highlights its potency. When believers unite in prayer, they create a spiritual synergy, amplifying their intentions and drawing closer to God's presence.

In the digital age, technology has also influenced the practice of prayer. Online prayer groups, virtual church services, and faith-based apps have made it easier for believers to connect and share their prayer requests, transcending geographical boundaries. "And if we know that he hears us—whatever we ask—we know that we have what we asked of him" (1 John 5:15). This assurance from John emphasizes the efficacy of prayer. Whether uttered in the quiet recesses of one's heart, spoken aloud in a congregation, or shared digitally across continents, every prayer is heard by God.

Nonetheless, prayer is not just about making requests or seeking relief from challenges. It's also an act of gratitude, praise, and ado-ration. In the hustle and bustle of modern life, taking moments to express gratitude through prayer can shift perspectives and cultivate a heart of contentment. "Enter his gates with thanksgiving and his courts with praise; give thanks to him and praise his name" (Psalm 100:4). This Psalm is a joyful exhortation to approach God with a heart brimming with gratitude. In the act of thanksgiving, believers acknowledge God's countless blessings, big and small.

In short, the role of prayer in modern life is multifaceted. It serves as a bridge between the temporal and the eternal, the indi-vidual and the Divine. In a world that often feels fragmented and overwhelming, prayer remains a unifying force, grounding believers in love, purpose, and divine connection. Through the lens of the Bible, Christians can appreciate the depth, richness, and transforma-tive power of prayer in their daily lives.

CHAPTER 9

The Christian Family in Today's World

The family unit, often described as the cornerstone of society has undergone significant transformations in the modern era. Amidst evolving societal norms, technological advancements, and shifting cultural landscapes, the Christian family faces both challenges and opportunities. The Bible, with its timeless teachings on love, commitment, and values, provides a guiding light for Christian families navigating the complexities of today's world.

"But as for me and my household, we will serve the Lord" (Joshua 24:15). Joshua's declaration underscores the centrality of faith in the Christian family. Regardless of external influences, the family remains a sanctuary where God's presence is honored and celebrated. In today's fast-paced world, families often struggle to balance work, leisure, and spiritual commitments. The demands of modern life can sometimes overshadow the essential task of nurturing familial bonds and spiritual growth. "Train up a child in the way he should go; even when he is old, he will not depart from it" (Proverbs 22:6). This Proverb emphasizes parents' pivotal role in shaping their children's spiritual journey. Parents lay a foundation throughout life by instilling Christian values from a young age.

The advent of technology has brought both blessings and challenges to the Christian family. While digital tools offer opportunities for learning and connection, they also present potential pitfalls, from screen addiction to exposure to inappropriate content. "All things are lawful for me, but not all things are helpful. All things are lawful for me, but I will not be dominated by anything" (1 Corinthians 6:12).

Paul's words to the Corinthians resonate in the context of digital consumption. While technology is a valuable tool, Christian families are encouraged to use it judiciously, ensuring it aligns with their values and doesn't dominate their lives.

The modern family also faces challenges in upholding Christian teachings on marriage, sexuality, and relationships in a society that often holds differing views. "Therefore, a man shall leave his father and his mother and hold fast to his wife, and they shall become one flesh" (Genesis 2:24). This Genesis verse highlights the sanctity of the marital bond in Christian teachings. In a world of evolving relationship norms, the Bible provides a blueprint for love, commitment, and fidelity.

Christian families also have the unique opportunity to be beacons of love and service in their communities. By practicing hospitality, serving the less fortunate, and building bridges of understanding, they can reflect Christ's love in tangible ways. "Let love be genuine. Abhor what is evil; hold fast to what is good. Love one another with brotherly affection. Outdo one another in showing honor" (Romans 12:9–10). Paul's exhortation to the Romans encapsulates the essence of Christian familial love. It's a genuine, selfless love that seeks the highest good for others.

The Christian family in today's world, while facing unique challenges, is also positioned for profound impact. Grounded in biblical teachings and fortified by faith, Christian families can thrive amidst modern complexities. By upholding Godly principles, nurturing spiritual growth, and being ambassadors of Christ's love, they can be shining examples of God's design for family in a rapidly changing world.

CHAPTER 10

Christian Leadership in a Secular World

In an increasingly secularized world, where religious beliefs often take a backseat to worldly pursuits, the role of Christian leadership becomes paramount. Leaders who embody Christ's teachings can influence communities, organizations, and even nations, guiding them toward values of love, justice, and righteousness. The Bible, rich with examples and teachings on leadership, offers invaluable insights for those called to lead in today's complex landscape. "Whoever wants to become great among you must be your servant, and whoever wants to be first must be your slave—just as the Son of Man did not come to be served, but to serve, and to give his life as a ransom for many" (Matthew 20:26–28). Jesus's words challenge the conventional notions of leadership. From the Kingdom perspective, true greatness is rooted in service. Christian leaders, therefore, are called to lead with humility, always prioritizing the needs of those they lead.

In the secular realm, leaders often face the temptation of power, prestige, and material gain. This allure can sometimes overshadow the core values and principles guiding decision-making. "For what shall it profit a man, if he shall gain\ the whole world, and lose his soul?" (Mark 8:36). This poignant question posed by Jesus serves as a reminder of the transient nature of worldly gains. Christian leaders are encouraged to weigh their decisions against eternal values, ensuring their leadership leaves a lasting, positive impact.

The challenges Christian leaders face in a secular world are multifaceted. Due to their faith-based stances, they often must navigate ethical dilemmas, societal pressures, and sometimes even opposition. "Be strong and courageous. Do not be afraid or terrified because of them, for the Lord your God goes with you; he will never leave you nor forsake you." (Deuteronomy 31:6) This assurance from Deuteronomy fortifies Christian leaders with the knowledge that they are not alone. Even in the face of adversity, God's presence is a constant source of strength and guidance.

Effective Christian leadership also involves building bridges of understanding and collaboration. In a diverse world, leaders can foster dialogue, dispel misconceptions, and work toward common goals. "Let your light shine before men in such a way that they may see your good works and glorify your Father who is in heaven" (Matthew 5:16). By exemplifying Christlike values in their leadership, Christian leaders can influence even secular environments. Their actions, rooted in love and integrity, can inspire others, and bring glory to God.

Moreover, Christian leaders are called to be visionaries, looking beyond the immediate to the eternal. They are tasked with the responsibility of guiding their followers toward a higher purpose, aligning their goals with God's plan. "Where there is no vision, the people perish: but he that keepeth the law, happy is he" (Proverbs 29:18). This Proverb underscores the importance of visionary leadership. Christian leaders, guided by God's Word, can provide direction, purpose, and hope to those they lead.

Christian leadership in a secular world is a journey fraught with challenges but also filled with immense opportunities. By grounding their leadership in biblical principles, Christian leaders can navigate the complexities of the modern world with wisdom and grace. They are positioned not just to lead but to transform—influencing societies, shaping cultures, and pointing people toward the eternal love of Christ.

CHAPTER 11

The Power of Forgiveness in Healing Relationships

In the intricate embroidery of human relationships, misunderstandings, betrayals, and hurts are inevitable. Yet, amidst these challenges, the Bible offers a potent remedy: forgiveness. This act, simple in concept but profound in impact, has the power to heal, restore, and transform relationships. Rooted in Christ's teachings and exemplified in His life, forgiveness is a cornerstone of Christian living. "For if you forgive other people when they sin against you, your heavenly Father will also forgive you. But if you do not forgive others their sins, your Father will not forgive your sins" (Matthew 6:14–15). Jesus's words during the Sermon on the Mount underscore the paramount importance of forgiveness in the Christian faith. It's not just an act of grace toward others but a reflection of the grace believers themselves receive from God.

In today's world, where pride and ego often dominate, choosing to forgive can be countercultural. The societal narrative often promotes revenge or holding grudges. However, harboring resentment can be a heavy burden, affecting one's peace, health, and spiritual well-being. "Get rid of all bitterness, rage and anger, brawling and slander, along with every form of malice. Be kind and compassionate to one another, forgiving each other, just as in Christ God forgave you" (Ephesians 4:31–32). Paul's exhortation to the Ephesians is a clarion call to release negative emotions and embrace a spirit of kindness and forgiveness. By doing so, believers align themselves with Christ's nature and foster healthier, more harmonious relationships.

Forgiveness, however, is not synonymous with condoning wrong or ignoring justice. It's about releasing the desire for revenge and entrusting justice to God. "Do not take revenge, my dear friends, but leave room for God's wrath, for it is written: 'It is mine to avenge; I will repay,' says the Lord" (Romans 12:19). This verse from Romans reminds believers of God's sovereignty in meting out justice. By choosing forgiveness, Christians free themselves from the cycle of bitterness and trust in God's righteous judgment.

The act of forgiveness also has profound implications for personal healing. When individuals choose to forgive, they embark on a journey of inner healing, releasing past hurts and opening their hearts to God's healing touch. "He heals the brokenhearted and binds up their wounds" (Psalm 147:3). This Psalm beautifully captures God's heart toward those who are hurt and wounded. As believers embrace forgiveness, they position themselves to experience God's deep healing and restoration.

Moreover, forgiveness strengthens community bonds. In a world rife with divisions, the act of forgiving can bridge gaps, mend rifts, and foster unity. "Above all, love each other deeply, because love covers over a multitude of sins" (1 Peter 4:8). Peter's words highlight the transformative power of love, which is intrinsically linked to forgiveness. When communities prioritize love and forgiveness, they cultivate an environment of trust, understanding, and mutual respect.

The power of forgiveness in healing relationships is immeasurable. Rooted in Christ's teachings and exemplified in His sacrificial love and forgiveness are gifts that believers can extend to others, reflecting God's grace. In a world that often magnifies hurts and offenses, choosing to forgive is a radical act of love, one that has the potential to heal hearts, restore relationships, and transform communities.

CHAPTER 12

Embracing God's Purpose
in Times of Trial

Life's journey is punctuated by seasons of trials, challenges, and uncertainties. For believers, these moments, while daunting, are also opportunities to delve deeper into God's purpose and draw strength from His promises. With its rich tapestry of stories and teachings, the Bible offers solace and guidance for navigating these tumultuous times. "Consider it pure joy, my brothers and sisters, whenever you face trials of many kinds, because you know that the testing of your faith produces perseverance" (James 1:2–3). James's words serve as a potent reminder that trials are not mere obstacles but refining fires. Faith is tested, strengthened, and matured through them; leading believers closer to spiritual maturity.

In the modern world, where success is often measured by material gains or societal accolades, facing trials can be disheartening. Yet, the biblical perspective offers a different lens, viewing trials as avenues to understand God's more profound purpose. "And we know that in all things God works for the good of those who love him, who have been called according to his purpose" (Romans 8:28). Paul's assurance to the Romans is a beacon of hope. Even amid challenges, God orchestrates events for the ultimate good of those who trust in Him. This divine orchestration, though sometimes beyond human comprehension, is always rooted in love and purpose.

Trials also allow believers to introspect and realign with God's will. In moments of difficulty, the world's distractions fade, allowing for a more explicit focus on God's voice. "I will instruct you and teach you in the way you should go; I will counsel you with my loving eye on you" (Psalm 32:8). This Psalm captures God's commitment to guiding His children. In times of trial, His voice becomes the guiding light, leading believers through the maze of challenges toward His perfect plan.

Furthermore, trials foster a more profound sense of community and interdependence among believers. As individuals share their struggles, pray for one another, and support each other, the bonds of fellowship are strengthened. "Carry each other's burdens, and in this way, you will fulfill the law of Christ" (Galatians 6:2). Paul's appeal to the Galatians underscores the importance of communal support. By bearing one another's burdens, believers embody Christ's love and fulfill His command to love one another.

It's also essential to recognize that trials are temporary. While they may seem overwhelming, they are fleeting moments in the grand tapestry of eternity. "For our light and momentary troubles are achieving for us an eternal glory that far outweighs them all" (2 Corinthians 4:17). Paul's perspective on trials, as described in the Corinthians is anchored in eternity. When viewed, considering eternal glory, the challenges of the present become bearable and purposeful.

Embracing God's purpose in times of trial is a transformative journey. While the world may view trials as setbacks, the biblical perspective sees them as stepping stones toward spiritual growth, deeper purpose, and eternal rewards. Grounded in God's promises and fortified by faith, believers can navigate life's challenges with resilience, hope, and unwavering trust in God's sovereign plan.

CHAPTER 13

Bridging the Gap: Navigating the Intersection of Technology and Faith

Enhancing religious practices in the digital age

In the ever-evolving landscape of the digital age, technological advancements have saturated almost every facet of human existence, including religious practices. The intersection of technology and faith expedites transformative changes, offering new avenues for engagement, connection, and expression of religious beliefs. However, while religious organizations need to welcome technological innovations, they must navigate the delicate balance between leveraging these tools for enhancement and ensuring they do not compromise the core tenets of faith. This final chapter intends to bridge the gaps between faith and modernity, exploring specific technological advances that have impacted religious practices in the digital age, both the benefits and potential challenges, and examining strategies for religious organizations to benefit from these advances without compromising faith, illustrated through concrete examples.

Technological advances impacting religious practices

Virtual religious gatherings. Video conferencing technology has revolutionized how religious communities gather and worship, transcending geographical barriers and accommodating diverse sched-

25

ules. Religious organizations now conduct virtual services, prayer meetings, and spiritual classes, enabling members to participate from the comfort of their homes. For example, during the COVID-19 pandemic, churches, mosques, and synagogues worldwide turned to platforms like Zoom and YouTube Live to host online worship services, fostering a strong sense of community and continuity amidst physical distancing measures, making the audience feel more united and supported.

Accessibility of religious texts. The digitization of sacred scriptures has democratized access to religious texts and empowered believers to study, reflect upon, and share their faith with unprecedented ease. Online platforms such as BibleGateway and Quran.com provide searchable versions of the Bible and the Quran, enabling users to explore specific verses, translations, and interpretations. Additionally, e-book readers and mobile applications offer portable access to religious texts, allowing individuals to engage with faith on the go, fostering a sense of capability and connection.

Social media and religious discourse. Social media platforms serve as dynamic arenas for religious discourse, community building, and outreach in the digital age. Religious leaders and organizations utilize platforms like Facebook, Twitter, and Instagram to share teachings, connect with followers, and promote religious events. For example, many hashtags facilitate collective prayer and solidarity during times of crisis, fostering a global sense of religious belonging. Moreover, social media enables individuals to explore and engage with diverse religious perspectives, promoting interfaith dialogue and understanding.

Religious education and e-learning. Technology has revolutionized religious education, offering innovative tools and platforms for learning and spiritual development. Individuals now have more avenues at their disposal to deepen their understanding of religious teachings and traditions simply by using online courses, webinars, and podcasts. Platforms like Khan Academy and Coursera offer classes ranging from comparative religion to theological studies, catering to learners of diverse backgrounds and interests. Additionally, digital resources such as virtual reality (VR) simulations and augmented reality (AR) apps enhance immersive learning experiences, allowing users to explore religious history, rituals, and artifacts in virtual environments.

Religious apps and digital tools. The proliferation of smartphones has led to the emergence of religious apps and digital tools designed to facilitate spiritual practices and religious observance. These apps encompass many functionalities, including prayer reminders, scripture readings, meditation guides, and virtual pilgrimage experiences. For example, apps like Pray.com and Insight Timer offer guided prayers and meditation sessions, while apps like Hajj App provide virtual tours and logistical support for pilgrims undertaking the Hajj pilgrimage. Additionally, digital tools such as online donation platforms streamline financial transactions and stewardship within religious communities, enabling members to contribute to charitable causes and support their faith-based organizations securely and conveniently.

Strategies for religious organizations to benefit from technological advances

Embrace technology as a tool for advancement. Religious organizations should view technology as a tool for enhancing, rather than replacing, traditional spiritual practices and teachings. While virtual gatherings and digital resources offer valuable opportunities for outreach and engagement, they should complement, rather than supplant, in-person worship and community interactions. By integrating technology thoughtfully into existing religious frameworks, organizations can leverage its benefits while preserving the authenticity and integrity of faith-based experiences. Virtual reality could be a specific strategy to enhance the experience of physical rituals or use social media to facilitate community engagement and outreach.

Cultivate digital literacy and ethical use. Religious leaders play a crucial role in cultivating digital literacy and promoting the ethical use of technology within religious communities. They should educate members about responsible online behavior, safeguarding personal privacy and security, and discerning reliable sources of spiritual information amidst the abundance of online content. Moreover, religious organizations can leverage technology to address contemporary ethical and social issues, such as digital inequality, online harassment, and misinformation, through advocacy, education, and community-building initiatives. By taking an active role in guiding the ethical use of technology, religious leaders can ensure that these tools are used in a way that aligns with the values and teachings of their faith.

Foster inclusive and accessible practices. Incorporating technological advances into religious practices should prioritize inclusivity and accessibility for all community members, regardless of age, ability, or technological proficiency. Religious organizations can achieve this by offering alternative formats for virtual gatherings, such as audio-only options for individuals with visual impairments or low-bandwidth internet connections. Additionally, they can provide training and support for older adults and technologically marginalized populations to navigate digital platforms effectively and participate fully in online religious activities.

Maintain sacred spaces and rituals. While embracing technological innovations, religious organizations must maintain sacred spaces and rituals that embody faith's spiritual essence and traditions. Virtual experiences, such as online prayer services and digital pilgrimage simulations, should always complement, rather than replace, physical acts of worship and communal rituals. By preserving the sanctity and symbolism of religious practices, organizations can reassure the audience about keeping their faith's traditions, ensuring that technology enhances, rather than detracts from, the spiritual depth and authenticity of religious experiences.

Conclusion

The digital age has ushered in many technological advances that have profoundly impacted religious practices, offering new opportunities for engagement, learning, and community-building within faith-based communities. By embracing these advancements thoughtfully and ethically, religious organizations can connect with the power of technology to enrich and strengthen their faith communities while preserving the timeless values and traditions that form the spiritual identity and expression bedrock. Religious organizations can navigate the complex intersection of technology and spirituality, ensuring that technology serves as a catalyst for deeper spiritual connection and collective flourishing in the digital age simply by striking a harmonious balance between innovation and faithfulness.

CONCLUSION

As we reach the apogee of our exploration into *Faith and Modernity*, I hope that this journey has been as enlightening for you as it has been for me. The intersection of faith and modernity is not a crossroad of conflict but an avenue of opportunity. It is a chance for us, as believers, to showcase the timeless relevance of the Gospel in a constantly changing world.

The challenges of modern society and technological advancements are not obstacles to our faith but platforms from which we can proclaim the love of Christ. Whether it's through digital evangelism, engaging with contemporary issues from a biblical perspective, or simply living out our faith in our daily interactions, we have the tools and the mandate to be salt and light in the world.

I am reminded of the words of the apostle Paul in 1 Corinthians 9:22, "I have become all things to all people so that by all possible means I might save some." Our approach to modernity should be adaptable without compromise and engage without dilution.

In closing, I'd like to express my heartfelt gratitude to my pillar of strength, my wife, Rolaine, and our five young men. Their unwavering support and prayers have been instrumental in this endeavor. To all the readers, I pray that as you navigate the intricacies of faith and modernity, you are continually guided by the Holy Spirit, finding innovative ways to share the love of Christ in our modern age.

May God bless you abundantly, and may you always find the perfect balance between holding onto our faith traditions and embracing the opportunities of the present.

In Christ's love,
Mario Joseph DBA, MSOL, BA, BAOL

ABOUT THE AUTHOR

Dr. Mario Joseph epitomizes a life transformed by faith and dedicated service. Since converting to Christianity in 1994, he has embarked on an unwavering devotion to God, family, and community. Married to Rolaine Joseph for three decades, their union has been blessed with five sons: Romario, Darnell, Rollinsky, Andrew, and Matthew.

Education has been a cornerstone of Dr. Joseph's life, earning him two bachelor's degrees in business administration and organizational leadership. Dr. Joseph's thirst for knowledge led him to pursue master's degrees in organizational leadership and biblical studies, further enriching his understanding of leadership in secular and spiritual contexts. Driven by a commitment to excellence, he attained a Doctorate in Business Administration, solidifying his organizational dynamics and management expertise.

Dr. Joseph's passion for youth development is evident in his roles as President and Founder of the Center for Youth Development New Jersey and Founder and Executive Coordinator of Epic Youth Nations (EYN) Ministry. Through these platforms, he tirelessly works to empower young people, guiding them toward purposeful lives rooted in faith and integrity. Beyond his academic and ministry endeavors, Dr. Joseph serves as President of Bethel's Board of Trustees and Administration, wielding his leadership acumen to steer the institution toward greater heights of success. He is also a licensed preacher, imparting spiritual wisdom and guidance to congregations.

A polymath in his own right, Dr. Joseph has honed his skills in various disciplines, including project management, digital marketing, and grants writing and management. His literary contributions to the Christian community are profound, with numerous authored books inspiring countless individuals on their spiritual journeys.

Dr. Mario Joseph's life is a testament to the transformative power of faith, education, and service. His unwavering dedication to uplifting others has left an indelible mark on all who have encountered him.

9 798892 436274